Why the Gods Don't Get It

Why the Gods Don't Get It

Poems by

Bill Christophersen

© 2021 Bill Christophersen. All rights reserved.
This material may not be reproduced in any form, published,
reprinted, recorded, performed, broadcast,
rewritten or redistributed without
the explicit permission of Bill Christophersen.
All such actions are strictly prohibited by law.

ISBN: 978-1-63980-067-4

Kelsay Books
502 South 1040 East, A-119
American Fork, Utah 84003
Kelsaybooks.com

Acknowledgments

The following poems, some slightly revised, have appeared in print as indicated:

California Quarterly: "Hominid Fossils Near Laetoli"
Chicago Review: "Hardanger Nocturnes"
Columbia Review: "Recon" (earlier version published as "Poem")
Connecticut Poetry Review: "Night Music"
cur.ren.cy (online literary journal): "Ayacucho," "Chalatenango"
Evening Street Review: "What I Heard"
Great River Review: "Dwarf Sea Horse"
Innisfree Poetry Journal: "Cuttlefish," "Dream of the Sown Seed"
Hanging Loose: "Going to the Videotape," "Where Love Goes," "Dreaming Knives"
Light: "Dogs"
Main Street Rag: "Excavation"
Montez Press at Mathew NYC (broadside): "Sparrow"
Rattle: "Neighbor"
Rhino: "Angel Wings, Keyhole Limpet…"
Right Hand Pointing: "West Side Story"
Robinson Jeffers Tor Foundation Newsletter: "Why the Gods Don't Get It"
Sierra Nevada Review: "Reading Hardy in the Tremont Library, 1971"
South Dakota Review: "Black Locust Haiku," "Rattlebox Moth"
Southern Humanities Review: "Fall"
Sundial: "Why I Am Underemployed"
The Beast in a Cage of Words: "To monitor the effects"
Yale Review: "Cocktails at the Millennium Hotel"

Contents

Forced Entry   13

Noir

Urban Pastoral   17
Dreaming Knives   18
Dancin' on the Third Rail   19
Reading Hardy in the Tremont Library, 1971   21
West Side Story   22
Lunar Eclipse   23
Subway, 4 a.m.   24
Cocktails at the Millennium Hotel   26
Sparrow   27
Dancin' with Daddy G   28
Kicking Back in SoHa   29
Chain Letter   30

Night Music

Traveling Angelica   37
Christmas Card   38
Sweetgum Haiku   40
Angel Wings, Keyhole Limpet . . .   41
Night Music   42
Missing You   43
Vertigo   45
Engaging the Snub-Nosed Eye   46
Going to the Videotape   47
Where Love Goes   48
Rappaccini's Garden   49
Hardanger Nocturnes   50
Three-Point Movement   51
Dream of the Sown Seed   53

Why the Gods Don't Get It

Hominid Fossils at Laetoli	57
Palm Sunday	58
To monitor the effects	59
Cuttlefish	60
Recon	61
Ayacucho	62
Dwarf Sea Horse	63
Chalatenango	64
Easter	65
Hyena	66
Ethnic Cleansing	67
Manhattan Fourth	69
Neighbor	70
Why the Gods Don't Get It	71
Excavation	72
No Country for Old Men	73
Rattlebox Moth	74
Columbia University: August 6, 1995	75
Pentecost	76

The Door

The Door	79
The Fumbled Ball	80
Why I Am Underemployed	81
Mi Casa Es Tu Casa	82
What I Heard	84
Every Time She Opens the Door	85
Apartment-Sitting	86
Fall	90
Dogs	91

Black Locust Haiku	92
Fifty	93
Death's Door	94
Notes	95
About the Author	97

Forced Entry

A sound, as of a
word bitten in half
by a harsher word; a
door slamming shut.
I'd been writing—
jimmying and
unlocking words.
Writing about
something fearful,
something part of me
wanted to let lie.
I rose, listened
at the door (heart
a gunned engine),
not sure what I
had or hadn't heard,
what wasn't or
was happening.

Noir

Urban Pastoral

It was after the war. Evil
had been chased back to its
Old World lair. In the
Bronx (its Dresden still
25 years off), young moms
would leave sleeping infants
in their carriages, unattended,
outside Macy's Parkchester
while they shopped.
For 45 minutes, an hour.
You'd see the buggies
all lined up, just
waiting for the bogeyman.

Dreaming Knives

When you're eight, a pocketknife enthralls. . . .
The "Pavilion of Fun" arcade in Coney Island
featured a glass display case with assorted
knives strewn on a gently conical field
whose apex was a hole.
                        Insert a nickel:
the field flush with pocketknives revolves.
Press a button: its motion stops; an arm
resembling the tone arm of a record player
arcs upward through the field. . . .
                        With all those knives
bunched up like sliders sunning on a rock,
it seemed the arcing needle couldn't help
but nudge one over the edge, into the breach. . . .
Damn! (Bad luck? Precision engineering!)

Dancin' on the Third Rail

Um-hm, I'm that kind of kid. . . . Hitch a ride
on the back of a bus, side of a subway car.
One time, yo, I made this life-size dummy—
crammed a shirt and jeans with old underwear,
stuffed a ski mask full of funky dishrags,
stapled it to the shirt, shirt to the jeans:
Pushed that sucker out the bedroom window
twelve floors above the plaza where the biddies
veg like crows on them varnished wooden benches. . . .
Went up the roof once, jimmied the metal door
to the whatchacallit, top of the elevator shaft.
Slid in, surfed a ride on an elevator car.
Don't dare me, Jack: I'm the kid walked the catwalk
on the Number 6 el from East 177 to Whitlock. . . .
See me hang by one hand from this fire escape?
I'm practicing, 'case I ever have to rescue
a baby in a fire, you dig? Crab-climbed
the hall in Lonzo's railroad flat, his shorty
mama hunting up and down for us while we
loafed up there for twenty minutes—flies
among the cobwebs, freeze-frame hurdlers, Pro
Keds' suction cups suctioned to the plaster. . . .
I'm the kid throws a pencil up to stick
in the cork-tile ceiling during Spanish, then
shoot it down with a rubber band, make it land
on the head of Señor Smartmouth. Lunch period,
I'm throwing them pats of butter up to the ceiling
so they stick—fall back down two periods later
in some fool's mash potatoes! . . . Yeah,
you know me: I'm the bad-ass bought a dog
just to have it eat my homework. I'm not cool:
I'm Cool Hand Luke, eat a bucket of raw eggs
to win a sucker's bet. I'm Wack the Slacker,

the kid they say, 'be sorry as hell someday,
big-rock jiver doin' permanent detention,
motto inked on my boosted loose-leaf binder:
"Send me to the principal already!!!"

Reading Hardy in the Tremont Library, 1971

In Thomas Hardy's Wessex, which, for all its
hay trussers, furmity vendors, ale-house bumpkins,
isn't so different from the Bronx (Darwinian
crucible, families persisting amid ruins), nothing
can be taken for granted. When lightning strikes,
some drudge of a milk maid or barley harvester
will be in harm's way, causing successive ripples
of hurt and hardship to radiate throughout
the neighborhood, though, chances are, someone
somewhere will gain by the incineration. Close
the book now. You've been warned. Uh-oh, is that
your tenement blossoming in flames?
Nothing to be done, I guess. The setting sun
(which Hardy likens to a drop of blood poised
on the eyelid of a hill) will go down, come up:
a one-trick pony. Its setting will tranquilize
or frighten you; settle you down or set your teeth
on edge. Peasant that you are beneath your spectacles,
you'll pray out loud, curse the broken street
that leads to still worse neighborhoods, through which
you're obliged to walk. Oh, you'll rally, try
not to flinch when the next bolt rends the sky.
The light show will subside until your tensed
muscles—well, you've read enough to know
the way such melodramatic story lines
resolve. Meanwhile, buck up! Take your cue
from the not-yet-shot-out streetlight whose mercury-
vapor beam transfigures the stripped sedan.
Bear in mind: The library offers shelter,
quiet, a sense of normalcy. You'll need to think
in such gobsmackingly basic terms, going forward.
Beyond the el, the sun's come up again:
a coin plucked from a snookered bookie's eyelid.

West Side Story

Outside the efficiency flat, domestic
arguments ricocheted in the air shaft.
We were 25, 26; got by on canned ravioli,
pork and beans. Joked about living
in the land of the midnight sirens. Hell,
that street at night? Black as a garrison belt.
We'd eat our supper and stay put. Dishes done,
you'd read your Rex Stout. I'd stretch out, sip
a Schlitz, watch the TV sets flickering
like pilot lights in the windows opposite.
Once from the fire escape a gloved hand
worked a chisel under the window sash,
you screaming at the blinds, crying
for the things that come, the things that don't.

Lunar Eclipse

We missed it. As the hour approached, a fog
rolled into town, turning ambient light
into caramel murk, a vaporous eggnog.
But we saw a lot of people out at night,
standing around in clusters on the street,
craning their necks and pointing, as if Superman,
accomplishing some civic-minded feat,
had just been sighted overflying Manhattan.
They called to mind people in a newsreel:
a bemused, not paranoid, metropolis;
a citizenry game enough to deal
with the portents and visitations in their midst,
unaccustomed to holing up at night, to feeling
outgunned, outnumbered, cowed, overshadowed, eclipsed.

Subway, 4 a.m.

No train comes. Rubbish
vogues on crossties as rats vie
for cantaloupe rind.

Token clerk yawns, nods.
Baby-faced hustler stoops, sucks
tokens from turnstile.

Alongside trash bin
on uptown platform: A match
flares in a cupped hand.

Cop weighed down by stocked
accessories belt belts down
bottled orange juice.

Bobbing amber light
resolves at tunnel's mouth: track-
walkers walking track.

Smashed cowboy empties
pack on floor of subway car:
tumbleweed ten-spots.

Broadway train pulls in
to Times Square. Forget Disney:
twenty cops, guns drawn.

Bag lady coughing
up pieces of lung in a
monogrammed hankie.

In the garbage bin's
wrapper-strewn penumbra: blood
spots, a blackened spoon.

End of platform: Rat's
eye glints red; piled trash bags do
the funky chicken.

Cocktails at the Millennium Hotel

"I'm secretly a dominatrix," hissed our host-
ess, having scolded her husband for dragging a chair
across parquet. (They're a Nick and Nora sort of pair.)
I laughed twice, after first mishearing most
of what she'd said with so conspiratorial an air:
"You're secretly a dot matrix, did you say?"
(We'd been talking about computers, about Y2K,
and the vodka tonic had snuck up unawares,
a thief in the night.) I tried—sipping hard—
to imagine what it would be like to *be*
a locus of points; a matrix; a virtual ghost.
"Molecular biologists," she deadpanned, "would agree."
I thought about hosts of nimble-witted PCs
wired for oblivion, and about a house of cards.

Sparrow

In A.D. 627, when the missionary Paulinus sought to convert Northumbria's King Oedwine to Christianity, Oedwine summoned a counselor for advice. The counselor, solaced by the promise of a heaven, advised the king to accept the Cross. As things stand, he ventured, a human soul is like a sparrow that flies in at one end of a mead hall, passes through it, then, seconds later, flies out through a far loophole into hibernal darkness. What have you got to lose?

I'm waiting on a lower platform of Manhattan's 59th St./Seventh Ave. subway station, a multitiered, cross-woven hub of tracks, stairwells and branching corridors, where rush-hour throngs surge beneath fluorescent lights and the escalating plosives of oncoming trains punctuate the din of white noise. On a cable above the express track is a sparrow. It twitters, then cocks its head for a response, a clue as to how to escape this caterwauling maze, as an uptown D rings for departure and a Brooklyn-bound A barrels into the station.

Dancin' with Daddy G

The curtain rises: You are eating breakfast.
The Goddess of Buttered Toast winks from behind a rock.
You stir your tea, wring out the bag and toss it in the fire.
The day begins to fit like a glove.

Invisibly, and as if to test our character,
isobars shuffle and realign above our noses.
We adapt, of course. We're here, aren't we? A spry metropolis
straddles a fault; love lingers; the twister twists away.

Or else it happens. You roll over, play dead,
die, fault yourself with a vengeance,
then crook one eye and squint through the dust:
A bird alights on a power line.

Survivors fly their kites and laugh.
"We in the East have gotten the West's weather."
The grounds crew rolls back the tarp and play
resumes, but first: some breakfast.

A finite series of breakfasts, and after that,
night to fall like a scrim, or strop.
We adapt, of course. We're here, aren't we?
You stir your tea, throw it in the fire.

Kicking Back in SoHa

And so I sit eating eight-dollar sorbet in a grungy-chic armchair just inside a new open-air cafe on Amsterdam between 122nd and 123rd, the heart of SoHa. That's "south of Harlem," in case you're not hip to New York's latest real-estate-industry coinage: a half-dozen square blocks of vermin-infested walk-ups cum co-ops, "charming prewar apartments" whose rents have suddenly gone the way of alphabet city's. The cafe is across the avenue from the spot where, one night twenty years ago, I was robbed, beaten and kicked by four teenagers—and almost dragged up to a rooftop in the projects for some more-leisurely entertainment. In those days the area was simply Harlem. No one had thought to christen its southwest corner with a trendy initialism that would make it ring invitingly in the ears of the young and monied, make it smack of art galleries and lofty-ceilinged bistros, make it seem somehow discrete from the ghetto that sprawls for miles north and east. It's pleasant, I'll admit, to know that tonight as the sun goes down and I stroll back to 121st, I probably won't run into the likes of the guy with the butcher knife who jacked up two seminary students in front of my building back in '87. Yes, of course I'm amused to see Spandex-clad Barnard girls go jogging blithely in Morningside Park, a place that used to be off-limits to anyone who wasn't packing. (Now profs' wives and their poodles haunt the dog run.) Far be it from me to wax nostalgic for dimly lit streets, burglaries, suspicious fires and crack vials littering the sidewalks. But, hey: eight bucks for a scoop of lemon sherbet?

Chain Letter

The first scary thing was
realizing I might know someone superstitious enough
to have forwarded it.

*

"Daisuke S. sent copies of this letter
to twenty people around the world.
Within a month, the municipal authority
promoted him to chief dispatcher." I
think about the elegance of the appeal; the
self-discipline of Daisuke—an inspiration and
admonition to lazy readers everywhere; the
fact that the writer chose to make his lead example Japanese;
the cachet of being chief dispatcher of something, somewhere.

*

English teacher that I am in one of my
half-dozen or nine lives, I
make copies, turn the silly thing
into a lesson on logic. It's all
there: shaky premises, Bible
quotes taken out of context,
false analogies. . . . My
students look at me like I'm crazy.
"Sonia S. put her copy of this
letter in her desk drawer and
forgot about it. A month later
she was hit by a bus and killed."
"Begging the question?" one student asks.
"Post hoc ergo prompter hoc?" another
ventures, textbook splayed.

"Bingo," I say, Cartesian pride
swelling my Western heart.

*

"What we supposed to do with these, professor?"
one student says after class. "What you gonna
do with yours? We all got to give them to twenty people or
who knows what happens?" "Whaddya mean 'we'?" I say,
making the obvious joke. She gets angry. Really angry.

*

On the way home, the whole episode
replaying in my mind, I
dodge a bus on Seventh Avenue, think
maybe I'm the fool here. The
chairman of the anthropology department
died in a restaurant a few
weeks ago. Heart attack. My
brother-in-law: just out of the emergency room after
disturbing a hornets' nest. He'd
taken up gardening for relaxation. Who knows
what causes what? Why
take chances?

*

I may as well admit that I'd
relish a promotion. A full-time
position, perhaps? (In the deep right field
of adjunct teaching, it gets late early.) Maybe
that was part of why I handed out the letter?

Then again, by now a stressed-out
Daisuke may be gulping sleeping pills, leaving
his wife, dispatching
himself. I'd like to write to him, see
whether he rues the day he
kept the chain unbroken.

*

My niece likes chain letters. For her
they're a kind of hands-across-the-water,
extended-family thing minus the hassle of
being a pen-pal. But with the added rush of maybe
making thousands of dollars
if everybody else ponies up 25 cents a letter, as
she's doing: It's a no-brainer, she says. Everybody
gets rich, nobody dies.

*

My Thursday students, skeptics all,
read the xerox and crack up. "Professor, you're
taking no chances, huh?"

*

Next week in my Wednesday class
a student asks me if I believe in God.
Sensing a trap, I do a tap dance about how
I believe there are realms beyond our understanding.
The student wags her finger, says I've begged the question.

*

I have. I do, though. Believe in God.
On certain days. For instance, the day after
four teens mugged me on Amsterdam Avenue at
11 o'clock at night. Back then I carried a
can of mace in my pocket for contingencies. Two of the guys
hammer-locked me, another took the mace from my pocket,
held it to my eye and pressed. It
didn't work. They had to use fists. Two of them
wanted to bring me to a rooftop where they could
take their time. I figured I had maybe five,
ten seconds of consciousness left. I say figured
because that's how it was: Some part of me was
hovering ten feet in the air, watching me get my
ass kicked, assessing probabilities. That bloodless,
limbic ghost—where did it come from? The leader
nixed the rooftop idea and said to make it quick. I was
spread-eagled against a car, by then. The parting kick in the nuts
landed an inch north of my left testicle. They grabbed my
wallet—an afterthought—and split through the projects. I
found my glasses and the luckily useless mace and
hobbled home. What, I said to myself the following day,
were the chances?

*

For several weeks after that, I
couldn't walk down the street without turning around completely
every fifty steps or so. Who knew what was coming up
behind? Superstitious? Well, not exactly, no. More like
a compulsive disorder. But isn't superstition a close cousin, a
sort of generalized version of the same? A scared, proleptic
maneuvering? An attempt to evade the worst, not let it
catch you off guard? Such traumas—our own,

those of friends, family—and our reactions eventually
link up, become a suit of mail we strap on
every time we leave the house. The most
reasonable among us, I'm guessing, do this
on some days.

*

"Professor," said one student a week before the semester
ended, "you're not going to believe this, and I
feel really foolish telling you, but
I sent out twenty copies of that letter you gave us and
I've been getting all this money in the mail. It's
making my mother very nervous."

Night Music

Traveling Angelica

At night
beside the Plains of Abraham
on the Governor's Promenade, overlooking
the St. Laurent and Old
Quebec's honkytonk mélange of
boutiques, cafes, saloons and
gimcrack tourist traps, a hooded
busker's fingertips trace circles
on the rims of sixteen crystal tumblers
(the sky a Maxfield Parrish painting
ripening into cobalt behind the
Chateau Frontenac's rimed spires):
"Moon River"
"Jesu, Joy of Man's Desiring"
Pachelbel's "Canon"—
ghosts coaxed, whistling, from glasses of water.

Christmas Card

A "Season's Greetings," smothered in pods,
hangs like breath in the air beneath the tree.
Below: a Mecca of minarets,
a snowy field, a rill turned to ice.
An ornamental border tapers off, as morning
rises on cuneiform pines. In the corner, a girl waves

to another in a scarf, who does not wave:
Back arched like a black-locust pod,
this girl trails a kite's tail of footprints. Morning
has lured her into a conflux of trees,
where she wonders if last night's snow will turn to ice,
encasing the whitened minarets,

the blue shadows of each minaret,
the contours of swept snowscape that wave
and fan above the maiden ice
girdling the ground's musculature. A pod,
brittle and shelled, the unlikely germ of a tree,
lies comatose at her feet in the frigid morning.

The girl in the foreground is whistling. "Good morning,"
she says to the onion domes and minarets,
tickled by their daft geometry.
"Crescent rolls dipped in waves,"
she quips, and "sugar cones, glazed with ice."
The other gapes, as pod after pod

wriggles like a hamster's nose. The sunlit pods
squirm collectively in the quickening morning,
reminding the addressee that this season of ice
is itself a bulb whose green minarets
lie dormant. (The addressee is trimming his tree,
strewing icicles light as radio waves

that move in unison, as convection currents waft
each bough.) What, meanwhile, has become of the pods?
They've exploded in a nova of microscopic trees
that vanish like meteorites in the snow. Next morning
everything freezes brilliantly. By now the minarets
have arranged themselves behind windows of ice.

Great lattices of ice condense in waves
that break against minarets, boughs reft of pods.
Christmas is over. Take down the tree.

Sweetgum Haiku

The sweetgum's pollen
swirls across the paving stones.
Newly minted stars.

Yellow-green, the bright
powder glisters like something
radioactive.

The sweetgum shakes its
unspooled, translucent leaves: What
fool is off to work?

Star-shaped leaf—sign of
teacher's approval: I fear
you inflate our grade.

Two grackles eye me
from the sweetgum's foliage.
Can't return their stare.

Angel Wings, Keyhole Limpet . . .

Muskmelon scent, breasts
like Anjou pears. Her
smile bleaches sheets, thaws frozen pipes.

Is that the new moon, or your pale
cuticle hovering over the Taconic?

She crooks a cheeky eye, and I'm
rye straw in a cat's-paw, a
shuttlecock in a hurricane.

For you I'm memorizing Saturn's moons, the
presidents' birthdays, the
cognomens of sea shells (Shark's
Eye, Lightning Whelk).

Name your whim: "Clue" by candlelight?
Colonel Mustard, at your service. With the candlestick.

Pick me up or put me down. What's that? Ha!
Pull the string, missie: I'm done with gravity,
delirious as a gyroscope.

Night Music

The new moon's tooth put to rout a perfect dusk.
Night settled in—a low-octave drone that grew
unsettling, then scarcely audible. The hours flew
backward, roosted like birds while the crescent tusk
lorded it over everything, its power
uncontested among the asterisks
of stars. At last a cat's-paw rank with musk
lured you into opening like a flower.
I tended you like a gardener on that bed
of black loam, that springy bed of pine-
needle-and-rabbit-warren earth, whose infrared
warmth radiated upward, much as wine
radiates up the chest cavity to the head;
tended, then entendriled you like a vine.

Missing You

1

Tonight all peace is the peace which passes understanding.
The tenements sweat, desire coursing the asphalt streets,
scaling the fire escapes, peering into windows. When you
left, budgets lapsed; a phone keeled over.

2

I see you in road signs; in country bars;
curled up in a cuticle of Mediterranean beach, or pining
quietly in a trilogy of Elizabethan novels.
By day you scissor-kick in mauve waters. By night
an empty space in the hollow of my hand whistles transatlantic
        lullabies.

3

What can I buy you? A yellow polo shirt? Seedless grapes?
Some French bread to knock rhetorically against a lamppost?
Would you like a box turtle? A turquoise scarab?
A diamond ironing board?
A thimble full of multicolored vitamins?
Several thousand miles of railroad track?
A fjord issuing in fishing smacks and maelstroms?
A microcassette of Quebecois fiddle tunes?
A lassoed asymptote?
The milk teeth of a nocturnal mammal?
The Kirlian photograph of a leaf?
Your own wind tunnel?
A Japanese print of dragonflies flying?

4
The plume is in my hand. My hand
is in your pocket. Every day
goes like a bean into a jar.

Vertigo

It was tough, that time you had to go.
Jujitsu works best, I told myself.
Turn your mind, like a penknife, to a project,
I told myself. (You told me that.)

All the same, it was tough. How tough? No worse
than a pulled groin muscle. (Don't be arch:
That's a sophomoric trope.)
Or a shaved face in a firestorm. (Nope.)

Let's try analogy, where the odds are better:
What ellipsis is to syntax, your simpleminded loan
shark smile in the medicine chest is to my breakfast,
my pair of pants, my inner ear. The TV waxed silly.

What to do, besides be snide. Fondue
was a stroke of genius: Sitting up in bed,
I'm a chef-d'oeuvre! My minted toothpicks
a handy heist, and a stitch in time

saves nine. . . . It's ten o'clock and I'm fine
but I need a country-western station,
a crystal set, an automobile radio: half a chance
to track the signal ringing in my teeth.

Next week you returned, your cochlea revamped,
feeling like a million dollars to boot,
simultaneously elbowing tea stains from sallow Formica and
making the tea that needed to be made.

Engaging the Snub-Nosed Eye

Jaws thrust, we stalked through a perfect dusk.
Nothing would dissuade or persuade you.
We stopped where resins oozed from an elm
some bug or blight had mangled like a tusk.
"Get a load of this burl," I gestured, feigning
a botanist's detachment. The exposed
grain whorled in the amber swale,
the ocean flushing almost out of earshot.
"Listen," I said. "We don't *have* to let entropy
win. . . ." You fixed me with a bulbous eye,
less daunting than the smirking razor, yet
a far cry from last month's Come-Right-In:
This one—unblinking, marmoreal—
perused me from the depths, a giant oyster.

Going to the Videotape

The Sturgeon Moon—green around the gills,
a midnight riser—drifts beyond the fire
escape's top rungs, the coils of razor wire
separating rooftops. I take two pills
to give sleep half a chance. Bent out of shape
by a beached affair, I pick the carcass clean;
replay each close-up of the breakup scene
I co-starred in last week. . . . The videotape
doesn't lie; yet its *cinéma vérité*
lapses oddly into Hollywood
cliché on playback. . . . Did I do and say
that? My histrionic gambits could
have been cribbed from *High-School Confidential*! Shucks!
The pain is real. How come the acting sucks?

Where Love Goes

Sometimes it goes out for a little walk
up and down your pusillanimous backbone.

Or burrows ingenuously into your hip
pocket. And leaves with what it finds.

Sometimes it takes a dive and is counted
out. The champ goes on thinking like a champ.

Or it goes, like hub caps, into a delinquent's
bedroom. The law gets involved.

Love breast-strokes its way into your best
friend's boat house, takes its time coming out.

Or disappears, then sprouts, green and slender,
through a crack in the I'll-be-damned sidewalk.

Once in a while, it goes as advertised: two
hang gliders riding the thermals above

the California coast, as manzanita seed pods
pop like pan-roasted corn on a Sierra mountainside.

Rappaccini's Garden

Exotic fragrances? They're better shunned.
The olfactory fuse is easily blown,
disorienting us, leaving us stunned,
enraptured. . . . Rappaccini, known
for practicing an occult botany,
grafted plants of such alluring smells
that visitors became unwittingly
enthralled by their intoxicating spell.
I've visited that garden; draped my nose
over this bloom and that until my vision blurred,
my throat and windpipe tightened. When I chose
to leave, I couldn't; to speak, my words were slurred. . . .
Beauty isn't truth. And I am done
with sensory overload, rule by pheromone.

Hardanger Nocturnes

1

An ocher sky ignites the spruces.
Petrels, all noise and wings, strafe the shore.
In the sun's wake, lobster smacks trawl the channel or
veer off into azure. A goat
bleats from the path, where foxglove, peat
and wind-pruned juniper conspire. At the foot of the fjord:
an island, "formed when a troll fell over backward."

2

Pitch snails glisten in the grass.
Ghosts leap from the fingers of trees, the phloem of sedges.
Across the fjord: a loon's arpeggios,
the wind in a fen, the
white noise of forests.
The neighbor's cow browses. An auburn moon
bends melodies from the blade of a ripsaw.

3

Night sharp as glacier-etched glass. In the wee hours
clouds trawl the fjord like submarines, their
engines muffled. Here and there in the pitch
a leaf explodes, luteins sprinkling the ground.
A hoarfrost's caught the squash—September's
prelude to white night and the sullen floes.
The East: taut colloid of lampblack and indigos.

Three-Point Movement

for Alain

The globe, the
conga drum, your
paper-lanterned ceiling light—
that's about all I can decipher
of the interior we watched Nick paint
on a piece of gesso-ed cardboard twenty years ago.
I still have it. You might remember
dark transverses and the tension between a
sea-green palette and three black oblongs—
negative spaces jostling in the picture plane.
Hints of a chair arm, I think, and French doors survive

And memories of the apartment we shared on 115th Street:
you with your film classes, your rap sheet of incompletes, your
women; me reading *The Spy Who Came in from the Cold* and
The Psychology of Education in the cat-clawed armchair.
The painting, you thought at the time, was nothing special
(though you asked Nick if you could keep it as a memento;
I fished it out of the trash the day you moved,
surprised to find you had tossed it). Special or not,
those dark-green clusters, that lime globe
seem now, like chlorophyll, to convert the past,
releasing it into the close air.

These days I live like a fish in a bowl, a
man nursing a perpetual cold.
And you? How's L.A.? Leena? the kids?
What kind of movie has your life become?
Nick is dead. Died of a stroke.
An art dealer upstate filled me in last summer.
So there's the news (and some of the weather). What
strikes me now are those rectangles he painted
while our eyes were occupied with the globe, the lantern:

parts of a plastic surface that day, they've
hardened into place beyond the picture plane.

Dream of the Sown Seed

I dreamed a moonless night, a ship at sea,
a cabin lined with claustrophobic berths.
It seemed a long time since we'd left the firths
of home—Mom, Dad, Granddad, me.
As the last watch tolled—six bells, three
o'clock—I rose to carry out my chore:
to read aloud a bit of the Gospel lore
that eased the sleepless sleepers through the wee
hours (for the dark hung heavy as wet wool,
never mind the lantern's amber pool).
It opened to the parable of the sower,
whose flung seeds went rolling here and there,
to be choked by weeds, thorns, rocks or to fare
well. The blast tossed the ship from swell to swell.

Why the Gods Don't Get It

Hominid Fossils at Laetoli

Sadiman boomed, and
damp ash captured the double trail:
footprints amid the random scratch
of guinea fowl. Now, as then,
whistling thorns stud the plain
where rain is scarce and Sadiman still smolders.

Palm Sunday

The cathedral a
music box, spring
unwinding. A
mob scene in the
insect world,
intimations of
flesh wounds to come.
Soon plots will
thicken, the ground
quicken and this
squirming in the
heart's warren segue
to Easter.

To monitor the effects

of nuclear explosions on eye tissue
they sent a remote-controlled plane carrying twenty rabbits
through a blast zone in Nevada.
The bomb went off on schedule, but
the test failed.
The rabbits closed their eyes.
So the experiment was repeated. This time
they sewed the rabbits' eyelids open.
But the bomb went off a nanosecond
late; the plane was vaporized.
So the experiment was repeated. This time
they sewed the rabbits' eyelids open and
reprogrammed the timing mechanism.
Everything went smoothly.
The rabbits came back blind.

Cuttlefish

Chameleon-times-a-thousand with a bill,
teeth, tentacles and suction cups,
this full-rigged cephalopod can summon up
the colors of a rainbow trout at will
or modify its shape to hide—or kill.
Now redeploying as a spear of coral,
now flattening itself to mime the floral
patterns of anemones, it trusts its skill
to fuddle barracuda on the prowl.
To hunt, it snakes an arm around the lee
side of a rock, or oozes through a reef,
decoying, lassoing, mantling in its cowl
the luckless prawn or sand crab. Whoa! See
its dark eye case that crevice like a thief?

Recon

Pinecones fall like
hand grenades around us.
Silent armies pass us in the night.
The twitch above your eye
talks a blue streak, brother, as
a breeze segues to feet fording
a stream I could just about
reach with a forward lateral. You
know the scream of blistered skin?
The taste of too-sweet tea?
We lie in the dark, bivouacked
among pinecones liable to
go off at any moment.

Ayacucho

They leave them by the road, mouths
stuffed with cactus, eyes
cut out: a people so dangerous
a bullet's too good

Dwarf Sea Horse

These ultra-faithful creatures mate for life:
a daily courtship ritual of synchronized
swimming, entwining of tails, mesmerized
dancing round a plume of sea grass. Strife,
that bane of earthly pairs, is tranced away,
and with it, procreative roles: The female
ejects her eggs en masse into the male,
whose sphincter-lipped brood pouch incubates
the lot, swaddled in a bolt of sperm.
The ova turn his swollen belly red.
Indefatigable, he'll carry them to term,
release them to the deep—then, having bred
five times in quick succession, breed once more.
Nine of ten hatchlings perish in the reefs offshore.

Chalatenango

The clinic's gone. Three Maryknoll sisters
raped and killed. Mercy itself the target.
A rogue brigade? Come on. *A Marxist cell?*
What kind of ideology is served

when national guardsmen mutilate a nun,
mail shorn extremities to a mother? Father,
shake the sleep from your eyes! Muster up!
The broken bodies fester in the sun.

Easter

Green covers gray
as paper covers rock.
Sunday-schooled, we
sang hymns, clutched
hyacinths, pocketed
forgiveness we
didn't need: blue
petals, nice
to the nose.

Hyena

There is a brazen prowler of the veldt
whose high-pitched laugh and sidling approach
signifies a rank intent to poach
a rival's kill. This scavenger's been dealt
a sorry set of looks: the brindled pelt,
matted gray and brown; the sloping rear,
hulking shoulders, outsized head and ears—
this skulking garbage can makes no hearts melt.
But when it comes to hijacking its share
of wildebeest carcass or impala haunch,
the sisterhood is powerful: even a pride
of lions will slouch aside and leave its fare
reeking in a cloud of flies, rather than launch
sorties against a gang of jaws this staunch.

Ethnic Cleansing

*They tell me death is plentiful
and everywhere, that all there is
is wall, table, gas-flame, bread . . .
things and their stubborn purposes.*
—Robert Winner, Flogging the Czar

Chintz window swags,
aluminum cot, half-empty
mug of tea—I've seen
trashier flats. Guys
get by with practically
nothing, you know? A
card table, oilcloth
tablecloth. Maybe
the memory of something
nice that happened once,
a cute babysitter, some
girl in a boathouse
—white flesh, water
lapping. Fact is, death
—this guy's, for instance—
is part of the package all
along: an unopened
box he's been using as a
night table. That's how I
look at it. The guy
was unarmed. There were
chevron designs
on the pockets of his
pajamas. Under different
circumstances? Sure,
we might have kicked his
ass, then taken him to
breakfast, asked about his
family, talked football, maybe
got his help solving one of those

officer candidates' school problems
about two trains traveling at
different speeds toward
different stations. But
circumstances? You
might as well say history.
History changes things.
Our dead uncles, cousins:
You think they didn't
drink tea, wear
stupid-looking pajamas?
Circumstances
are what everything
is about, you know?
It's why we
popped this meatball.

Manhattan Fourth

for John Hartman

The heat broke after eight. We paused to rest
on a bench beside a wooded stretch of park.
In front of us, a hill sloped down toward West
Harlem, and as dusk gave way to dark,
a firefly glimmered somewhere to our right,
followed by another. "Look up!" you said.
An aerial show of celadon taillights
blinking, tracing contrails overhead . . .
Then the rockets of the fireworks display
on the East River commandeered the show,
upstaging bioluminescence, till the fray
of cherry bombs detonating below
and police choppers scrambling from Hell's Gate
to the Heights quashed our urge to celebrate.

Neighbor

Thanksgiving Day, 1983.
The three of us are sitting down to eat
when D. recalls Mr. Breuer down the hall
in 2A. He lost his wife two weeks ago
to cancer, and it seems the neighborly thing
to ask him in to share the meal. Grief
has tenderized his face. He doesn't talk,
pushes a fork through the sweet potato squash.
The bruise on his arm resolves, on second glance,
into numbers. Yes, he says, he'd been interned.
At Belsen. He'd survived. *But what,* he asks,
*is "survive"? Is survive that your body
gets up, goes to window, goes to toilet,
makes tea, makes toast?* "Shovel this latrine,
Jew," *the German soldier says.* "So give
me shovel," *I says.* "There is no shovel, Jew,"
he says. "Use your hands."
                    *And so, is true,
Femmie and me survive,* he says, crying.

Why the Gods Don't Get It

From half a mile away, the four-car
pile-up looks like tumbling dice. You
don't hear much: some pings and pongs, a
residual tinkle like wind chimes.
Scan a schoolyard from a fifth-floor window:
You'd be surprised how much a knife fight
resembles a game of steal the bacon:
the clockwise circling, arms extended;
the crouching feints; the crowd of clenched
fists; the thrust.   Step back.
Turn down the sound. Pain
grows painless. The hooded Palestinian
whose bones the soldiers are breaking
outside the village wall; the *Honeymooners*
sitcom unspooling inaudibly in the
window across the air shaft—Ralph's
jacket is off, he's smacking Alice's
face with the back of his bus driver's
hand. What lousy acting, you're
thinking, as she crumples.

Excavation

We vacuumed it; we peeled it back like
layers of burnt skin, hovering above
raked dirt with lens and forceps. We
were here once: sometimes brutalized;
sometimes scapegoated, enslaved;
sometimes besieged; betrayed by spies
in our own or a neighboring camp; our cattle
slaughtered, wells poisoned, orchards
torched, huts gutted, daughters ravished,
children led away captive. What
possessed us so to persevere?
What limbic wont or fired will
supervened to keep us shaping clay
amphoras, planting winter wheat?

No Country for Old Men

Forget the birds in Euclidean trees.
Let the burnt-out filaments stay burnt out.
Take the powdered eggs away; instead,
the lady has ordered an idiot's wrist.

Forget the teakwood artifacts. Choose
platinum oar locks and liquid natural gas.
Sell short; invest in an all-purpose knife,
a ball-peen hammer: Italy's gone bankrupt.

Forget the slide trombone, of course.
Plan on canned pears, canned string beans, canned corn.
A picnic. Where's the all-purpose knife?
For music: the sound of a broken wrist clapping.

Break a leg. Grow lean as a wrist in splints.
Don't scruple to exercise a woman's prerogative.
This burnt-out troubadour is putting out to sea,
where the filaments of certain idiot plankton are constant.

Rattlebox Moth

If the name recalls the snake whose strident tail
freezes hikers in mid-stride, that's not amiss:
Although it lacks the rattle, fangs and hiss,
this moth that as a caterpillar feeds
on toxic rattlebox (a sort of killer pea)
is protected by the poison chemical kiss
it blows the approaching spider—a cartoon twist
on Nature's usual porno-gothic tale
of predator and gossamer-winged prey.
But (Darwin would have howled!) in order to stay
so adaptatively obnoxious, the female
needs a booster shot of toxins from the male.
Which she acquires every time she breeds:
His sperm's an essence of pesticide and seeds.

Columbia University: August 6, 1995

Dusk steeps above the quad.
An ocher moon illuminates the marble
stairwell, the mimosa's seed parachutes, the library's
Ionian facade. Day-Glo Frisbees skim the air.
An Asian girl in headphones lounges by the fountain.

Fifty years ago our fathers
struck a match: A new sun
rose where a city was. Miles
away in suburban train stations, flesh
peeled like paper from commuters' faces.

Let this pillar of
fire we conjured
go before us, no
more to be doubted
or believed in.

Pentecost

This is the time when you revealed yourself
to a stunned knot of frightened fugitives.
I too am frightened; speechless. The police
are armed for war. Our security forces
torture; terrorize. Prisons overflow.
And the flame that danced inscrutably on old
men's skulls burns but does not consume.
When you bid the skeptic thrust a fisher's hand
into the hole that was your side, you conferred
a boon: the power to speak; to be crucified.
I too want a boon; a tongue; consummation;
proof of the bloody hole; piece of the cross—
or a stone to mark the place that smacks of nothing.

The Door

The Door

For all the history of grief,
An empty doorway and a maple leaf.
—Archibald MacLeish, "Ars Poetica"

The open doorway frames a view.
Beyond, whispering grasses stand

in lieu, perhaps, of someone's grief.
Say it's so. You pass a hand

through it: Now it's yours. The poem
—opaque as night-entangled trees,

dumb as moss—has done its part;
has shown you the door. The rest is art.

The Fumbled Ball

The fumbled ball smolders in the mitt.
The panned debut is a play that never closes.
The just-missed train now and forever noses
into the station—where, again, you're missing it.

The fight you picked; the fight you should have fought.
The blows that failed to even up the score.
Flirtation you began and then forbore.
The love you feigned; the love you should have sought. . . .

I once heard terror brimming in a word
scissored by the closing of a door.
Or fancied it? I listened several more
minutes. That quarter note was all I heard.

Why I Am Underemployed

Shitcan the snapshots of apricot suns:
Someone is requisitioning hospital beds for Europe.
I have no experience; type quickly, with lots of mistakes,
uncertainty making my fingers doltish.

My attention wanders. I need to channel self-hatred
deliberately, like an acolyte; to brush with any available toothpaste;
to ignore the weather and other precious correlatives:
the linden tree's pale underclothes. . . .

Would a class ring open doors? Is love
a liability? a ploy? a perquisite?
Can I get by on fewer hours of sleep? Mom?
You who were a peasant in sweaters, once.

The subway speeds to its destination
full of murderers, mathematicians.
Civilities are flouted. What's up with that?
I daydream a lot about audiences.

Mi Casa Es Tu Casa

with Alain Berger

Here's the key—take it. I'm letting you use my
apartment. Actually, my memory of an apartment.
A memory I've embellished—as I invite you to do.
A place to crash, on occasion, now that your marriage
is the gift that has stopped giving and your job's
an ash tray full of spent cigarette butts and the kids
have gone from cute to annoying to alien and life's
an exercise in alternate-side-of-the-street parking. . . .
Take the key. Open the door.

Walk down the unlit hall past the kitchen and
part the beaded curtain. Enter the studio, its air
smelling of sandalwood. Not the kind of place
you were expecting? Right. Take a moment to
orient yourself. The décor: a rug—maroon with
black arabesques; sheepskins on the floor in the
corners; a sofa, on which a doffed djellaba half
covers a splayed volume of Larbaud; a low table,
at the center of which is a candy-bar-size slab of
Lebanese hash on a chipped saucer; alongside it,
joss sticks, a chillum, matches, two candles, a tea pot
and a tin of loose Darjeeling. From the ceiling hangs
a Moroccan lamp, its filigreed metal frame silhouetted
by an orange bulb. The lamp's upper and lower housings
are joined by a short, hexagonal chimney graced with
glass panels—red, green, orange—whose tones, like
the shadows of the filigree, play on the walls. Clay
drums and wooden flutes lie among the sheepskins.

Take off your coat. Light the candles. Care for a
pipe? Some tea? Watch the smoke curl, the steam
rise like the ghost of a scarf. . . . What time is it?
Midnight? Half past? No matter. See the wax,
how it pools. . . . Have you ever played drums?
flute? If the belly dancer should stop by, let her in.
She's not a whore. Pour her some tea. After a while,
pick up an instrument. If she dances, watch her dance. . . .
You've got the key now. Take care not to lose it.

What I Heard

For three minutes I'd
listened at the door,
not sure if what I'd
heard was what I
feared I'd heard. It
was. Hours later
the cops used my phone
to call in the report. A
push-in. Perp had
taped her mouth, tied
her arms and legs to a
chair, cut her clothes off,
raped her with his gun,
left by the door. No
witnesses. It was
all about power,
said the cop on the
phone. Everything's
about power, said
his partner, if you
scratch it hard enough.

Every Time She Opens the Door

You say you get used to this kind of thing
and you do get used to a lot of it, but,
you don't get used to this. The bar fights,
the gangbangers, the drugs, the heists, the
schoolyard shit that spills out onto the street,
yeah, sure. That don't faze me much.
Blood. I see blood every day, never mind
all day Saturday, the brass got me workin'
overtime like two years ago. Not this.
She could be my daughter, you know?
Well, not really, cause I ain't Asian, but
you follow me. What you think she's
thinkin', this filth pulls a knife, ties her
to a chair? starts cutting off her blouse, her
whaddya call that skirt-pants thing she's
wearin'? What's worse,
'Guy's doin' this to her where she lives.
We don't have a crime on the books called
felonious fright, but if I'm mayor, I'd
have 'em write one up. Even if this
slimebucket never tied her up, never put
a finger on her, just stood there lookin'
down, playin' mumbledypeg with the
knife in the floor, you follow me? Raped
with a gun? That girl'll never be the same.
She'll spend the rest of her life peein' in her
pants every time she opens the door an'
every time she closes it behind her.

Apartment-Sitting

Nosy as an in-law, I
check out the premises, browse
the bookshelves, test the bed,
then feed the pets, talk
to the plants, make a pot of tea.
It's 10 p.m.—still early. I read
awhile from a dog-eared
copy of *Evangeline,* my
changing eyes grateful for
the piano lamp's bright light.
Below on Amsterdam a
truck brakes. Quiet
follows, save for the
hamster rooting compulsively
in the wood chips.

     *

Hoping my own apartment in a
dicier neighborhood isn't being
similarly gone through in my absence, I
open the fridge, pop some Chinese
leftovers into the microwave, watch
the dish of noodles revolve behind
tinted glass. In the fish tank on
the countertop, the goldfish
smack their lips, sucking
food specks from the water's surface.

     *

Homemade baubles, crayon drawings . . .
The refrigerator is festooned with stuff.

I pour hot water over a cold teabag and wonder
why the fish named Mrs. Heffalump is keeping
so still. . . . Perhaps it's an emergency, the
sort of thing I'm supposed to be watching out for?

       *

The Mrs. flicks her tail. I ease
into the chair that looks like a velvet
satellite dish in a wicker frame. On TV
a white man in a breechcloth is being
chased all over Africa. Serves him
right, the colonialist dog. Isn't
this the life?

       *

Four a.m.: Where
am I? What's that low-
decibel sucking noise?
Where are the wife and
kids I never had? How
did I get here?

       *

Worked for a prestigious
magazine once. Had a
career simmering like
pork and beans in a pot.
I hate pork and beans.

Opened a can of something
else. Ever watch
canned food cook? It
makes you appreciate lids.

*

Nursed a terminal crush, an
interminable grudge. Had
a friend once who said,
"Maria likes me, guess
I'll go out with her." I said,
"You like her, huh?" He said,
"Point is, she likes me." Some
guys know how to get by.

*

Keep moving, I told myself, not
always knowing what I meant.
Keep reading, writing, working,
giving a hoot, I think. (I'm
a whiz with that sort of
buck-me-up balderdash.)
What I meant, though: Don't
get suckered by the TV,
sidetracked by the old
movies, lulled by the
clock's monotone.

*

My friends return, all
good will and gratitude.
I welcome them back, the kettle
whistling, part of me still
bolt upright,
bushwhacked,
running for my life.

Fall

for my parents

It doesn't please the way it used to please.
Not that the air's less crisp or less distilled,
October's breeze less optimally chilled
than that of autumns past; or that the trees
are any less tricked out in apricot-
ochers, the brakes of sumac less afire
along the parkway. Not that the entire
vegetable world, from bittersweet to box-
elder, hasn't come, kindling, into its own,
or that the orchards, branches weighted down
with apples to be pressed, put up, munched, milled,
are any less tantalizing this time round.
But as the folks grow haggard and housebound,
the season cuts much closer to the bone.

Dogs

They know us and they love us. Or they act
as if they know and love us, making
plaintive guttural noises, looking
solicitous or simply listening with tact,
or seeming tact, to our woes, suspending
judgment (as spouse or lover never can),
then insisting we get off our duffs, get on
with things, step out with them for a rousing,
buck-me-up walk in the park. Why not? We go,
give the benefit of the doubt to their sympathy,
their rescue mission disguised as Nothing at All,
old pal, old bean, old porcupine, old roomie,
'Just trotting by your chair and, well, you know,
I thought it might be fun to toss this ball. . . .

Black Locust Haiku

The locust's leathery
seed pods litter the sidewalk:
October's favors.

Half-turned leaves—their still
green veins temporarily
preserved in amber.

The bronze leaves fly. The
gold ones quake as if they know
what's in the offing.

Up top: two last pods—
commas punctuating fall's
runaway syntax.

Leaves, seed pods—gone.
Asbestos sky. The locust's
burnt-out filament.

Fifty

Wiser? I don't know. Eventually
self-interest makes us take a few precautions.
Health insurance. A fire extinguisher
for the kitchen. I've even learned to eat
my vegetables. (Milk's another story.
I take calcium pills to keep from looking like
a bishop's crook lamppost by the time I'm 65.)
Life's puzzles? Still in pieces on the floor:
Career. Love. Belief. The jig-sawed shapes
others assemble—mixed up, scuffed up, lost.
But one lives, fulfilled or unfulfilled, espoused
or un-espousing. One goes to sleep, gets up,
gets dressed, makes tea, burns the toast. One abides
the clutter underfoot. Or sweeps it out.

Death's Door

It's unmarked, of course,
a gunmetal rectangle, the
gray paint peeling. You've
passed it without noticing
more often than not (sky
a blue plate, schoolkids in
Day-Glo backpacks waiting
for the light to change, one
stooping to retrieve a dropped
hand-held). Death's door
is slightly warped and
frequently ajar, though if
you lean against it, it won't
necessarily open. Toss
a ball against it: the ball
bounces back. The knob's
a dull brass. There's no
keyhole, lock, intercom,
mounted light fixture.
Just a slight recess in the
brick housing. One day
you'll stop there to make
a call, wait out a storm,
and, with any luck,
nothing at all will happen.

Notes

"Cocktails at the Millennium Hotel": (1) Nick and Nora: characters in Dashiell Hammett's *The Thin Man*. Their breezy, alcohol-fueled domestic patter counterpoints the mystery Nick, as detective, hopes to solve. *The Thin Man* became a movie by the same name, starring William Powell and Myrna Loy. (2) Y2K refers to a mathematical malfunction that was widely expected to wreak havoc with the computers running everything from airplanes' operating systems to building management systems as the millennium arrived.

"Dancin' with Daddy G": Daddy G is the nickname of a tenor saxophone player celebrated in two hit songs from the early 1960s—"Quarter to Three," by Gary U.S. Bonds, and "The Bristol Stomp," by the Dovells.

"Rappaccini's Garden": The title image is drawn from Nathaniel Hawthorne's short story "Rappaccini's Daughter."

"Hominid Fossils in Laetoli": (1) Laetoli: a site in Tanzania made famous in 1976, when archeologist Mary Leakey discovered 3.7-million-year-old footprints preserved in volcanic ash, attesting to human ancestors who walked upright. (2) Sadiman: the name of the volcano near the site.

"Ayacucho": A city in south-central Peru, the site of atrocities committed by the country's military against people suspected of aiding or being members of the Shining Path guerrilla insurgency in the 1980s.

"Chalatenango": The title names a province in El Salvador where, on December 2, 1980, the described atrocity took place. The province was the site of several such atrocities committed during the civil war between U.S.-assisted governmental forces and FMLN guerrillas.

"Neighbor": Belsen: a Nazi concentration camp in north Germany.

"Why the Gods Don't Get It": The poem was a prize-winner in the Robinson Jeffers Tor House Foundation Poetry Competition, 2002.

"No Country for Old Men": The title is from the first line of Yeats's poem "Sailing to Byzantium."

"Columbia University: August 6, 1995" commemorates the bombing of Hiroshima half a century earlier. Physicists at Columbia, as part of the Manhattan Project, helped develop the atomic bomb.

About the Author

Bill Christophersen was born in the Bronx and educated at Columbia University. He is the author of *The Apparition in the Glass: Charles Brockden Brown's American Gothic* (University of Georgia Press) and *Resurrecting Leather-Stocking: Pathfinding in Jacksonian America* (University of South Carolina Press), as well as four previous poetry collections—*Two Men Fighting in a Landscape* (Aldrich Press), *The Dicer's Cup* (Kelsay Books), *Tableau with Crash Helmet* (Hanging Loose Press) and *Where Truth Lies* (Kelsay Books). His book reviews and critical essays have appeared in *Newsweek, The New Leader, The New York Times Book Review, The American Book Review* and *Poetry*. His poems have won awards from *Kansas Quarterly, Rhino* and the Robinson Jeffers Tor House Foundation, and have been nominated for a Pushcart Prize and for inclusion in *Best New Poets 2014*. He lives in New York and plays traditional and bluegrass fiddle.

www.ingramcontent.com/pod-product-compliance
Lightning Source LLC
Chambersburg PA
CBHW032009080426
42735CB00007B/549